SHADING SPIRITUAL
SIGNS & SYMBOLS

An Adult Coloring Book

by Authors
Lyn Ragan and Dorothy Pigue

To our Guardian Angels,
With Love and Grace...

Other Books by Lyn Ragan

Wake Me Up! a true story
How Chip's Afterlife Saved Me From Myself
fb/wakemeupbook

We Need To Talk
Living With The Afterlife
fb/weneedtotalkbook

Signs From The Afterlife
Identifying Gifts From The Other Side
fb/signsfromtheafterlife

Signs From Pets In The Afterlife
Identifying Messages From Pets In Heaven
fb/signsfrompetsintheafterlife

Other Books by Lyn Ragan & Dorothy Pigue

Shading The Colors of Grief and Healing
An Adult Coloring Book To Help Heal Through Grief
fb/shadingthecolorsoflife

Coloring The Shades of Grief and Healing
A Teen/Young Adult Coloring Book To Help Heal Through Grief
fb/shadingthecolorsoflife

Introduction

Lyn Ragan lost the *love of her life* in 2008. One second they were chatting on the phone and in the next, he was murdered while preparing for work.

Her grief spiraled into a web of sadness she found difficult to break free of. All of their future dreams destroyed and her life altered forever, Lyn was taken by surprise when she started receiving communications from her deceased fiancé— via dreams. Ms. Ragan would later write about their visits and eventually publish several books on the subject of *Afterlife Communications*.

Her mission in life is to help those who grieve from the loss of a loved one; her ultimate goal to replace painful grief with belief and understanding. Lyn works tirelessly helping those she can reach to understand this physical life is not the end of who we are, and that love and life does live forever— as do our Souls.

Dorothy Pigue was born into a family of clairvoyants. As a young child, she began hearing the voices of spirits around her. It took many years for Dorothy to realize she could communicate with the spirit world and with loved ones who have crossed over. Wanting to enhance her gifts and psychic abilities, she trained with Carl Woodall at the *Atlanta Metaphysical Center* in Atlanta, Georgia, and became a graduate of *The Anastasi System of Psychic Development* in 2014.

Dorothy is also a Master Herbalist who has been practicing as a Korean Medicine Woman since 1996. She is a Clinical Certified Hypnotherapist, a Certified Usui/Holy Fire Reiki ® Practitioner, and an aspiring author.

Dorothy's mission in life is to share her gifts and abilities in hopes of removing the *pain of grief*. Healing begins with love and from the other side, *Love* is the message she enjoys sharing.

Authors Lyn Ragan and Dorothy Pigue are excited to come together on a personal undertaking to help bring peace, love, and healing into the hearts of those who grieve.

Our Wish For You…

*E*very sign and symbol is important. Universal symbols and signs are the language of the Soul. They're also the language of Dreams. Throughout recorded history, signs and symbols have left lasting impressions in the hearts and minds of many.

Our wish is to help you become aware of, and identify, the various spiritual symbols you may receive or witness. That is why we produced this coloring book. Each page has a descriptive word or phrase attached to it. They are as follows:

hamsa hand; the lotus flower; the yin yang; the flower of life; the tree of life; the green man; the cross; the celtic cross; peace sign; the om; buddha; the turtle; day of the dead; ganesh; sun symbol; bastet; the griffin; metatron's cube; infinity; chakra; koi fish; hourglass; the pig; elephant; the bat; the beetle; the deer; the frog.

From our personal experiences, we believe each one of these statements is a dynamic blueprint toward acknowledging and witnessing signs and symbols.

Signs are normally very gentle. By their given nature, they do not demand a response nor do they direct us to take an action. Through their appearance however, we are given a spiritual reveal or quite possibly, a suggestion to change our course in life. This is where your intuitive awareness is most effective in understanding how to claim the message, or the meaning, in your sign or your symbol.

Just by coloring, studying, and gazing at the complexity and the deeper meaning each one of these illustrations holds within, we learn to feel connected, alive, and intrigued.

One step, one day, and one coloring page… at a time.

Hamsa Hand

Symbolizes "The Five Books of Moses"
or the five books of the Torah;
Genesis, Exodus, Leviticus, Numbers and Deuteronomy.
The Hamsa Hand is a protection symbol
against the evil eye and brings its owner
good fortune,
happiness,
luck,
and health.
It is also sometimes called "The Hand of Miriam".

Hamsa Hand

The Lotus Flower

*This stunning flower emerges beautifully
in the morning and then retracts at night.
The Lotus is associated with the sun
because it too disappears into the night.
The Lotus represents
spiritual awakening,
eternity and purity.*

Lotus Flower

The Yin Yang

Symbolizing harmony and balance
within the universe, the Ying Yang
exists in everything around us.
One cannot exist without the other.
They are opposite in nature,
but attract each other.
The Chinese believe that Ying Yang forms the
five elements believed to create the universe.
The five elements are
water, wood, fire, earth and metal.

Yin Yang

The Flower of Life

Considered to be the most sacred of all geometry

symbols, the Flower of Life radiates a pattern of

meaningful beauty and true elegance.

The Flower of Life can be used

as a tool during meditation.

Some people believe using the symbol

on electronic devices can help

diffuse harmful frequencies.

This exquisite symbol reminds us

that we are all

connected to each other.

Flower of Life

The Tree of Life

Rooted in the earth and reaching high for the stars,
The Tree of Life is created by the forces of
Fire, Earth, Air and Water combined.
From fire comes the power of the sun...
receiving living light.
From Earth comes the nourishment to the roots...
roots and sun combine to render giving power.
From water comes the power of life...
that will allow the fruit to grow.
From air is an exchange from the environment...
allowing the tree continue to mature and grow.
The Tree of Life symbolizes
immortality,
continued growth,
and the healing of the soul.

Tree of Life

The Green Man

*Symbolizing life rebirth, The Green Man
represents the cycle of growth every spring.
It is also a symbol of life and nature.*

The Green Man

The Cross

The Cross is a representation of the
crucifixion of Jesus Christ.
There are many different meanings of the cross.
Christians use it as a symbol of their religion.
Some people believe wearing one, or hanging one
in the home, protects from misfortune.
Many also believe that all four
physical elements make up the cross.
(Earth, Fire, Air and Water)

The Cross

The Celtic Cross

The symbolic meaning of the Celtic Cross

is faith,

hope,

honor,

life,

unity,

balance,

and transition.

A symbol representing the meeting place

of the Divine Energies, the center of the

cross-section is the energetic touchstone where

a concentration of cosmic power resides.

The Celtic Cross

Peace Sign

The peace sign symbolizes universal peace.
It was created by Gerald Holtom,
a British artist, in 1958.
The peace sign is internationally known
and became very popular
during the Vietnam War.

Peace Sign

The Om

The Om represents creation,
the oneness of all creation, and God.
This symbol is used in Buddhism and Hinduism.
It is also called Pranava, which means,
"it infiltrates life and runs through our breath."
The Om today, is practiced as part of Yoga.

The Om

Buddha

Buddha means, "The Awakened One"
and represents Siddhartha,
an Indian Prince who gave up the throne to seek
truth and the meaning of happiness for all mankind.
Buddha's teachings is known as the Dharma.
The followers of Buddha devote their lives
to the practice of Enlightenment.

Buddha

The Turtle

The turtle is a symbol
of the continuation of life,
persistence,
longevity,
protection,
innocence,
strength,
and endurance.

The Turtle

Day of the Dead

(Día de los Muertos)

*The Day of the Dead is celebrated annually in Mexico.
This spiritual festival honors the spirits of
departed loved ones who are believed
to return to earth to join in the celebrations.
The Skull Candy is one of the symbols
of the Day of the Dead.*

Day of the Dead

Ganesh

Ganesh is believed to remove
selfishness,
narcissism,
arrogance
and obstacles.
Ganesh is a Hindu god
that is loved among many Hindus.

Ganesh

Sun Symbol

The sun is the ruler of the higher self.

It represents growth,

passion,

power,

health,

and the cycle of life.

Sun Symbol

Bastet
"Cat Goddess"
Bastet is the Goddess of
protection,
pleasure,
fertility,
and motherhood.
Bastet is also a symbol of grace and poise.

Bastet

The Griffin

The Griffin combines the symbolic
qualities of the lion and the eagle.
Griffins symbolize wisdom,
strength,
salvation,
vengeance,
and the sun.

The Griffin

Metatron's Cube

Sacred Geometrical symbol.

It forms a map of creation.

The spheres represent the feminine

and the straight lines represent the masculine.

The weaving together creates oneness

of the two combined.

"We are all One."

Metatron's Cube

Infinity

Infinity means never ending possibilities.
It is a never-ending loop that represents
forever and always.
The infinity symbol is limitless of space and time.
It is a continual motion that expands beyond all
form and has no beginning or end.
Love is Infinite.

Infinity

Chakra

There are seven (7) centers of
Spiritual Power in the human body.

<u>Base or Root Chakra</u>
(last bone in spinal cord) RED, Prime, Power
<u>Sacral Chakra</u>
(ovaries/prostate) ORANGE, Creativity, Exploration
<u>Solar Plexus Chakra</u>
(navel area) YELLOW, Intellect, Perception
<u>Heart Chakra</u>
(heart area) GREEN, Connection, Growth
<u>Throat Chakra</u>
(throat and neck area) BLUE, Clarification, Expression
<u>Third Eye Chakra</u>
(pineal gland or third eye) INDIGO, Perception, Depth
<u>Crown Chakra</u>
(Top of head) VIOLET, Awareness, Being

Chakra

Koi Fish

The Koi fish is a common symbol
in both Chinese culture and feng shui.
The Koi fish is very powerful and can swim
against currents and can travel upstream, too.
The Koi fish symbolizes ambition,
good fortune,
prosperity,
courage,
success,
longevity,
and perseverance.

Koi Fish

Hourglass

The hourglass represents
continuous change,
life & death,
and balance.
It also represents the beginning
of a new phase in a person's life.

Hourglass

The Pig

The pig represents

good fortune,

luck,

wealth,

and prosperity.

The pig is also used in making piggy banks

because it represents saving and gaining wealth.

The Pig

Elephant

The elephant represents

patience,

honor,

stability,

and strength.

It also represents

good luck,

good fortune,

and protection in some countries.

Elephant

The Bat

The bat represents letting go
of the old and bringing in the new.
Bats are also symbols
of initiation
and transition.

The Bat

The Beetle

The beetle symbolizes

progress,

persistence,

stability,

simplicity,

security,

and protection.

The beetle is connected to the core of the earth

and represents groundedness.

The Beetle

The Deer

The deer symbolizes innocence
and true peace on earth.
They also represent a promise of
peace within and around you.

The Deer

The Frog

The frog represents awakening
your authentic truth.
It also represents eternal beauty within.
Just like the butterfly,
the frog symbolizes transformation.
Frogs bring magical blessings and prosperity.
It is also the symbol of true love.

The Frog